WAKING UP THE WEST

RETURN TO DREAMTIME

STEPHANIE HREHIRCHUK

Edited by
MARAYA LOZA KOXAHN

Copyright © 2021 by Stephanie Hrehirchuk

All rights reserved.

No part of this book may be reproduced in any form or by any electronic or mechanical means, including information storage and retrieval systems, without written permission from the author, except for the use of brief quotations in a book review.

Contact the author at www.StephanieHrehirchuk.com

This book is intended to entertain the reader. The author specifically disclaims all responsibility for any liability, loss, or risk, personal or otherwise, which is incurred as a consequence, directly or indirectly, of the use and application of any of the contents of this book.

This book is **memoir**. Some names have been changed and some **dialogue** has been recreated. All through the lens of insight and love.

Editor: Maraya Loza-Koxahn

Cover Design: Margarita Dimova

Interior images from Canva

ISBN:978-1-9991300-7-7

ISBN: 978-1-9991300-8-4(ebook)

For all the great dreamers
It's not always an easy path to follow your inner guidance and trust in a greater intelligent field. It takes equal parts courage and not giving a shit what others think about your choices.

THE DAWN

"The moth symbolized change and transformation. An insect of night, of moonlit life, dreamtime, the moth emerged amidst the group, waking in spring, as if to acknowledge our collective waking, our transformation, that we too held the ability to change the dream, to navigate within the darkness, within shadow, and always find sources of light. Just as the sun set, she flew off to explore the great nectar of night and dreamtime. She would see the dawn before the rest of the world. Was that something we could share with her?"

— Excerpted from *An Accidental Awakening: It's not about yoga; It's about family*

DEAR READER

If you can open or deepen your connection to Dreamtime, it will forever change your life. Whether it is forged during sleep, in the depth of meditation or communion with nature, this channel will serve both you and the world. For over ten years, I have spent nearly every morning on my front step. Usually in meditation. Often in contemplation. Most happily in pure observation and communion with nature and self.

The sky is insulated with falling snow or fragrant with coming rain. It's filled with the oranges and pinks of sunrise or luminescent white clouds that prompt me to ask, "Are you seeing this, Michaelangelo? You would love this sky."

Raven's call reverberates through my soul. Chickadees wake. Then sparrows. Magpies follow. Little brown mouse tunnels under the snow or sits and chews on grass roots.

Earth wakes before the world. I like that. The space before lights flick on in kitchens. Before cars start or children rush to school. Before the dog-walkers and the joggers. I like when it is just her and me.

I came here for her. The crispness of March air while the

sun's rays strengthen. The heat of August early in the day. White rabbit moves near. The sound of a hundred seagulls' wings whoosh above my head. There is a window of wisdom, of magic, on my front step.

I *feel* every whisper of breeze, every caw, every wing's flap, and every coyote's howl as if I were the source. For that time, those moments on my front step, I am complete.

Here, I take you through many of those magical moments. I give you the wisdom that was given to me when the window opened round and full on my step. And I sprinkle them with insights from dreams and meditations. We're done thinking our way into our future. To flourish as a civilization, we must return to Dreamtime.

June 20th, 2017
Summer Solstice morning

I open the front door. There is a large black and brown butterfly on the doorframe near my feet. I watch her. She feeds herself bits of whatever she finds there, something I can't see.

She moves outside to my doormat and continues to find food. She seems to be gathering nourishment from my front step. I grab my journal and pen from their hiding spot in the entryway bench and join her.

INTRODUCTION

April 26, 2020

Khali, my 12-year-old daughter had this to say at the dinner table tonight:

"How do I know that you are all real? What if we're really dreaming right now and life is just a dream? What if, when we die, we wake up?"

That's quite the contemplation over a plate of pasta. What Khali showed was that we all think about Dreamtime, daytime, nighttime at some time in our lifetime. What if what we believe to be real isn't actually real? What if what we believe *isn't* real has reality sewn into it?

How do we pluck the gems from Dreamtime? How do we discern wisdom from visions? What is the nature of a nightmare? If we don't ask the questions, how can we invite the answers?

After my year of yoga, retold in *An Accidental Awakening: It's not about yoga; It's about family*, a window opened to

Dreamtime. I couldn't write fast enough to record the strange, wild and wonderful world that I stepped into.

We have a gift in the West, many of us, this gift of privilege. Roshi Joan Halifax said it best in a March 3, 2020 Upaya article after her arrest while protesting climate change on the steps of the Capitol with the formidable Jane Fonda during a 'Fire Drill Friday':

"You can fall asleep, you can fall prey to your own unhappy story, and you can squander the precious opportunity to turn the light around and illuminate your mind, illuminate your heart, and discover how to end the suffering in this world. I urge us all to take responsibility for the privilege that we might have and use it well. I urge us to use our time well."

WE ARE fortunate and perfectly poised to potentiate a new future: for humanity and the planet. But we cannot do this using old mindsets and models. We must dream a new path forward.

It is time that the West wake up and return to Dreamtime.

Waking up the West is an account of my own process of entering the dance with the Dreamer, how it led to lessons with Albert Einstein on my front step and later as a compass to navigate pain and grief.

What incredible insights are waiting for you just the other side of the veil? I can't wait for you to find out. I look forward to the West waking and returning to Dreamtime.

I don't have it all figured out. Even after *An Accidental Awakening* and *Awakening on Purpose*, you will see here in this book that I don't have it all figured out. I'm less and less convinced we are supposed to. But still, the mystery unfolded itself in front of me and every cell in my body wanted to play. The woman, however, the wife, the mom, Stephanie, still lost her shit from time to time.

Over the years, I'd gotten comfortable with the chakras and familiar with nature's language, but Dreamtime ... Dreamtime twisted me like salt water taffy on a hot day. I jumped in with both feet, which made walking in two worlds difficult. Often, I fell back into the waking world, while trying to make sense of the dream world.

I learned many lessons from my years with the Dreamer. Insights came that my mind could never conjure. But I also learned what happens when you spend too much time in Dreamtime, and why it is best to work with a teacher or a dream guide.

Dreamtime is not only available in sleep. It includes daydreams, visions, spontaneous insights, communication with Nature, sudden inspiration, synchronicities and ah-ha moments.

It is my intention here to weave a web of Dreamtime, daytime, dreamers and possibilities, so that you, dear reader, begin to connect with your creative source and pay attention to your Dreamtime. My hope is that as we return to this yin source, we find the opening: the gateway to a harmonious and prosperous life on Earth.

> "...the role of the imagination must be cultivated and valued in this new world we are creating."
>
> — JEAN HOUSTON, THE WIZARD OF US

FROM ME TO YOU

Be grateful every day
    for our time here is short.

PART I

WHO AM I?

1

THE DREAMER AWAKENS

2013

Christmas morning, I open the gift from my kids: a journal, deep purple with two birds perched on a flowering tree branch. I run my hand over the soft faux leather cover and then open it to stare at the fresh blank first page. *What will be written here?*

A year of dreams, comes the answer. *I will record my dreams and see if there are indeed messages inside. I will play in the dream world and try to decipher its code. Perhaps I, too, can connect to the wisdom the Achuar people know in their dreams.*

I continue to think about the Achuar people, one of the world's last remaining dream cultures, introduced to me at the end of my year in yoga through the Awakening the Dreamer, Changing the Dream symposium. For an entire village to wake early and set the tone for their day by their collective dreaming – there had to be something there. And it wasn't only the Achuar who lived by dream guidance. Other cultures, like the Australian Aborigines, referred to Dreamtime and dreaming the world into being.

It was, however, the dreams of the Achuar people that led them to reach out to their American neighbours for help as they dreamed their village, their environment and their way of life destroyed by these same neighbours. To share their sacred and private way of life, to call out for help, they must have believed strongly in the messages of their dreams.

On the inside cover I write:

> *Dream Journal*
> *This is how we connect.*
> *This is how we communicate*
> *This is how we co-create*

With an indigo cover like sixth chakra, the journal conjures all-things Dreamtime. I sift through its pages at the kitchen table the next morning, poised to write, when a bald eagle flies low past my window. His immense presence stirs the air around me and my pen moves across the lined page. I capture the following words before they flee my mind.

> There is a difference between seeking and curiosity. Seeking holds the promise of a reward: we seek hard for the antidote to our suffering. Curiosity provides an Ah-ha! Gotcha! Just for the sake of getting ya. The curiosity of childhood provides no anticipated outcome, only scratches the figuring-out of the mystery in question. It's more *Let's see where this goes* than *What does it all mean?*

> Seeking is an adult's burden: grasping for an answer to an identified problem. Parameters are already set, expectations

> in place, form identified. Curiosity allows for any imaginable and, more likely, unimaginable outcome: even the possibility of no outcome. Curiosity is raw, spontaneous, organic and expansive. Seeking is narrow, focused, planned, with attachment to outcome.

> Curiosity is sitting in meditation with a smile on your face, noticing your position, your breath, thoughts, the process, the experience. "How curious!" you say. Seeking is sitting in meditation determined to get something from it: a nugget or treasure for doing it *right*.

I put down my pen and read what I've written as if hearing it for the first time. I realize I've spent many years seeking. Even now, I sought the messages of Dreamtime. I pick up my pen again and conclude the journal entry with:

I want to be curious.

2

THE RANT

JANUARY 24TH, 2013

"I'm not saying don't be strong." I paced the living room carpet while the spontaneous rant gushed from my lips. "But check your definition of strength. It takes immense strength to allow yourself to be vulnerable, intuitive, graceful, and soft. It takes creativity and strength to maintain your softness and display your vulnerability to the world while protecting that softness from those who judge, criticize or take advantage."

I stop to face myself in the large mirror above the couch. Both speaker and audience, I am alone in the room, save for my twelve-year-old cat. The Rocky Mountains stand in the distance out the window over my shoulder.

"I think we are missing the essence of the feminine. I've read that in meditation the act of trying to calm the mind is actually more doing, therefore not truly meditative. Similar to the return to feminine: less is more. We are feminine in our nature. It exists without our trying, striving and proving. This is not he versus she, not masculine versus feminine, not men versus women. We all hold masculine and feminine energy yet have lived in a highly masculine-centric world for a long time. A return to the feminine helps us restore the scales of balance that have tipped too far for too long."

Captivated by this stream of consciousness, I return to my pacing and allow it to continue. "I see many strong, empowered women yet their energy and actions are heavily masculine. They speak of intuition and spirituality, they speak of recovering the feminine, yet their actions follow old processes, systems and thoughts: more striving, achieving, reaching."

"Feminine power appears to lie in mastery of the subtle, the formless, the beauty, and emerging creativity. What is actually created is less important than the process. The masculine is in the finished product, what purpose it serves, how much it is worth. The feminine is in the blossoming, the formless. What is created is less important to the feminine than the flow, the rhythm and the possibilities."

"It may be difficult to allow the vulnerable, the intuitive, in a world where harshness still exists. Where anger and fear are prevalent. If we are truly to allow the feminine to re-emerge, to filter through civilization and nurture blossoming creativity, we need to protect it, to hold it sacred and honour it in each other. The feminine is the great creative, the masculine is what draws it into form. We have exhausted the old form. It is time to create anew."

"Find the strength that is not required to push further, work harder, yell louder, move faster or climb higher. Find the strength that fosters softer, slower, simpler, more elegant, beautiful and creative solutions, heightened intuition and connection to nature's rhythms. Find the strength in nurturing self, family and community. The strength in listening deeply for another way."

I collapse into the chair in the corner of the room. Rants

are equal parts exciting and emptying. The information runs quickly off my tongue and leaves me spent.

3

THE GRANDMOTHERS - DREAM

JANUARY 25TH, 2013

I am with many grandmothers. They want to do more, but we tell them to nap, to stay and rest. They are too old and weak. My grandma wants to walk with us to get ice cream. I tell her it is too far and will bring her back something, a long popsicle. I forget to bring it back for her.

There are two grandmothers in bed. My daughter, Khali, lies between them but she keeps moving around. I take her out of the bed so the grandmothers can get some rest.

When I wake, I am sad and disappointed in myself for not remembering the popsicle for my grandma. I grab my journal from my nightstand and quickly scribble the details of my dream before it fades. I feel like the grandmothers need to rest yet we are not responsibly taking up the duties they left to us. What are our duties? Grandma only wants to come for ice cream, a simple pleasure. We are not saving the world, just a walk for ice cream.

There is a sense of life's joys: ice cream, a small child cuddled in bed. There is also a sense of not allowing the grandmothers to do more, to do what they want. We are protecting them, but should we instead invite them to help us. Invite them along for ice cream. Allow them to support us. The grandmother: wise feminine energy. Perhaps instead of forcing them to rest, we can invigorate them by inviting them to come along for the walk.

4

A STONE BY ANY OTHER NAME

JANUARY 31ST, 2013

I hadn't visited the gem store in years. I'd actually forgotten it existed. My dear reiki friend and healer, Sophie, had suggested I pick up a new crystal to work with.

As I enter the shop, I remember why I'd forgotten about it. "Good morning." I smile at the store owner behind the counter. She looks up at me and says nothing. Prickly. I move on to the display cases. A tarot card deck catches my eye. I pick it up and read the back. *Focus, Stephanie. Just a crystal.* I was known to drop a small fortune in this type of store. I return the deck to its shelf. A stone next to it appeals to me.

"Excuse me," I opt to engage the not-so-chipper owner since I am the only person in the store and the awkward silence needs to break. "Can you tell me what this stone is?"

"Bring it over here."

Seriously? Are you trapped behind that counter? Do I need to call for help? Be nice, Stephanie. I pluck the stone and walk it over to her, placing it on the counter.

She looks over her glasses at it. "It's a fire agate."

"Really?"

She looks again. "Yes, that's a fire agate."

"Are you sure?"

She turns her gaze to me. "Quite."

"Hmmm." I pick up the stone and return it to its shelf, trying to make sense of it. I am no stone expert but something about the name feels wrong, as if the stone whispers otherwise. I leave the store, stoneless.

At home, I try looking up the stone but have no luck identifying it. Each day for a week, I google various possibilities, looking for a match. I can't get the stone out of my head and, for some reason, have to discover its rightful name.

I finally return to the store. The shop owner remembers me when I enter.

"I looked up that stone after you left to discover it was not a fire agate but a

poppy jasper."

It's funny that she also felt the identification wrong, as if the stone demanded we get it right. I still feel her research is incorrect but purchase the stone anyway as I know it's mine. It chose me last week, just as my rescue cat had chosen me twelve years earlier. This stone wants my attention.

At home, I take a deeper research dive into jasper, despite the migraine building behind my eyes. I finally find the markings match that of ocean jasper. *That feels right.* As a bonus, a suggested meditation accompanies the research. I read it over. It involves the bathtub: timely.

While the pressure moves alongside my head to the base of my skull, I head upstairs to run a tub. I take the ocean jasper with me into the bath, holding it in my hand. "Okay, ocean jasper." I sink into the warm water. "Thank you for granting me a vision." The stone obliges and quickly produces what feels like a past life and a revealing account of life in between lives. I close my eyes.

I stand on the top of Courthouse Rock in Sedona. There are two of us. I believe there was a fire but it is out now. I know I failed at my task but I don't know what exactly my task was. I only know I have returned to the village with it unfulfilled.

My Chief, Elder or superior stands atop the rock with me. His headdress is fuller than mine and I kneel before him. I am disappointed that I have failed but I accept my punishment of death as it is our way. I am a peaceful man.

My Chief or Elder is Leo. He ends my life, possibly with a blow to the head or a beheading. Then he and I sit, as spirits, side by side, legs dangling off the edge of the great red rock, looking over the beautiful expanse of Sedona before tourists or buildings or development. Great red rocks of Cathedral and green shrubs of agave and creosote dot the landscape.

We talk about how we'll be back for more adventures together. More lifetimes. I chuckle and say, "It'd be nice if next time we are on the same side."

5

PERMISSION TO QUIT

FEBRUARY 7TH, 2013

I want to take a course by Toko-pa called Dream Walking. It starts next week. The course is $150. I cannot afford to cover the cost since product sales have been slow.

I read an article yesterday by Martha Beck on quitting. Quitters are both healthier and wealthier it seems. It's all in the letting-go, knowing when to quit, when to "stop throwing good money after bad." Quitting almost always feels like a relief to me. And if I release my concern for what anyone else thinks, almost becomes always.

Quitting, for me, is an opportunity to let go, to lighten up and reinvent myself. It's my shedding-of-the-skin. Leo, during our recent group meditation, suggested I may shed my skin this year. Perhaps four times, like the southern rattlesnake. I liked the sound of that. Seasonal shedding suited me. Like the hat of the consultant, it fits me well. I don't enjoy hanging on to things that have served their purpose, particularly jobs.

When I think about what I'd like to quit in my life right now, I think about the company I started in order to sell my herbal oils. I love playing around with the plants, crafting the oils and coming up with new blends. The marketing and selling is dragging me down and I beat myself up because it's not as successful as I thought it should be.

I feel tied to it because of the investment of time and money. It feels like an obligation. I consider *obligations*. I create many of them. I set myself up for daily posts for social media, a series of ongoing classes, or a new yoga studio to carry the oils, then later dread the same obligations I create for myself.

I am quitting the company. Whew. That was a toughy. The whole website needs to go away. For now I will remove the products page. No more selling. No more marketing. No idea how to recover my investment but at least the good money won't follow the bad. Some things are never meant to be made into a business. They are purely personal. I need to step out from behind the counter and stop selling.

I delete the page. Funny thing: immediately after making the decision to stop trying to get people to buy the oils, three people emailed me about buying the oils. Now that I've made the decision, I can't wait to be done with it.

I reply to the email orders, opting to fill them, and quote the amount owing for each person. The total sales from the three clients is $148. I sign up for the Dream Walking course.

6

MIND THE WORK

FEBRUARY 9TH, 2013

"Use the mind to work, not to judge," come the words on the breeze. Struggle is a constant companion these days. My mind is busy.

I've tried to quiet my mind, observe it. It's difficult. Perhaps the best course is to direct it: work not judgement. I focus on my heart and return to my meditation.

My heart centre feels warm. It feels as if it is radiating heat. I sink deeper into meditation.

Let the heart lead to the work, then use the mind to work, not judge.

7

THE FOOL

MARCH 8TH, 2013

The Seed Event takes place in Calgary, bringing several of my favourite teachers to me in one venue. I opt to go alone and buy myself a VIP ticket to enjoy preferred seating and dinner with the speakers. I have no questions for them. I'd spent six months learning from the evocative Dr. Jean Houston through her telecourse and was a diligent student, practicing the work and doing my homework and research for myself. I simply want to thank her and tell her the incredible synchronistic opportunity that opened up directly after, and I believe as a result of, her course.

I just completed David Wolfe's online course of Raw Nutrition. I also have no questions for him. Again, I did my homework and integrated many of his teachings in my daily life. I simply want to hear him speak live, as I've enjoyed his energy nearly as much as I've enjoyed Jean's.

On my own at the event, I have little opportunity for verbal diarrhea. I chat briefly with a lady in the seat next to me, but in the absence of a close friend or colleague, have no outlet for mindless chatter. My attention falls fully on each presenter and I receive new insights and inspiration from my existing teachers as well as those new to me.

Strangely, the day keeps placing me face to face with these inspiring people. And each time, I find I have nothing I truly want to ask or offer, or that it isn't the appropriate time. My mind grows more and more restless with each encounter. I keep my tongue in the washroom alone with Dr. Houston, washing our hands. I am, however, unable to keep my tongue with David Wolfe.

Several times during the day, people hand me their phones, asking me to take a photo of them with their favourite presenter. I happily oblige, feeling no need to have one taken myself. I linger in the lobby after the dinner and notice David Wolfe enter and chat with those in the room. My mind decides I should take advantage of the opportunity and have a photo taken with him. I approach David just as he begins speaking to another. I patiently wait, striking up a conversation with a woman who happens to be the event photographer. She offers to take the photo of David and me.

I sidle up to David, asking for a photo. We do the customary photo lean in and smile for the camera when my mind, uncomfortable with the silence, feels the need to offer up something.

"I'm taking your Raw Nutrition Course," I say. "I love the format. It's like I live with you."

Well, there isn't much to be said after that, other than I want to find a hole in the conference room floor and bury my head in it.

I head back into the main room for the keynote speaker, Sri Sri Ravi Shankar. Thank goodness I didn't find myself face to face with Guru Ji. I can only imagine what fascinating tidbit would have escaped my mouth. I happen into the Mayor, who, coincidentally I attended grade three with - and proceed to share that fact with him, babbling on with a thank you for the great mayoring he was doing. Ally McBeal would've been proud.

By this time in the event I feel exhausted, not from the length of the line-up of speakers, but from my internal wrestling match between the wise woman and the fool. I line up to have my book signed by Dr. Houston, and take that opportunity to briefly and energetically thank her and tell the story of how her course and her teachings inspired me. As I drive home, I think of how often I speak to gain approval, or exert my will over another's, to be noticed or ... some sense of self-importance or fear of lost opportunity prompts me to fill a silence that I was otherwise content to enjoy.

> A wise man speaks because he has something to say; **a fool because he has to say something.**
>
> — PLATO

8

A LESSON IN DISCERNMENT

MARCH 20TH, 2013

I pull a spread of cards at the spring equinox, as I've done each solstice and equinox for the previous three years. My dearest friend gifted me with a spiritual journal on my birthday during our maiden voyage to Sedona. I loved that journal and followed the card spread suggested within its artistic pages.

Years out of date, I kept the journal so I could continue to reference the card spread details. There is a central card in the layout: the essence of the season for me. For this particular season, I happen to pull *Discernment*. It is a card I've pulled before yet the term still feels vague to me. Discernment. According to Google, it means "the ability to judge well." How exactly does that translate into daily life and, more importantly, how is it the essence of the lesson I need to focus on for spring? How will I know if I judge well?

I contemplate the word, roll it around on my tongue and in my mind. I settle on "making higher choices" as the guide to live by, but discernment seems more than that. As is often the case with seasonal card-pulling, once I forget about the spread and the details, I will certainly realize the lesson by the season's end whether I intend to or not.

A few weeks later, I discover that a Rinpoche is coming to visit Calgary. I read up on the Rinpoche. I can't help but feel he is an important person and that I need to attend. Looking at his picture, I am immediately drawn to the weekend seminars. Truth be told, the Rinpoche's dark eyes and beautiful face draw me. I forward the event details to my friend, Anna, who humorously addresses him as "His Handsomeness."

"Only you, my dear, would find the best-looking teacher," she teases.

As I enter the building for the event, many warm smiles from the small Buddhist community greet me. I take a seat and listen intently to the Rinpoche's words, taking several pages of notes. I am humbled and grateful to have the Rinpoche share his wisdom and warmth with me over the course of four lectures in two days.

Listening to him speak about the teachings remind me of listening to any of my favourite teachers speak on their subjects (whether Ayurveda, yoga or writing) with such love, appreciation and simplicity, as if their subject is a living, breathing being. Even if I didn't enjoy his affection for and knowledge of his teachings, I could not dispute them since everything he spoke of makes perfect sense to me.

It is the final lecture. A friendly fellow strikes up a conversation. "Do you study? What brought you here?" he asks.

"I recognize when a great teacher comes to our city and I believe it's important to support them," I reply.

"How do you honour a teacher?" The fellow continues to lean over the back of his chair in front of me.

"By *hearing* what he has to say," I reply.

"By practicing his teachings," the fellow corrects me in a manner that suggests he has been told this very thing, perhaps by his teacher. He is clear to point out that there are two groups, two styles of Buddhist students here. I do not wish to disparage him as he is doing his best, and our conversation produces many thought-provoking revelations; however, our exchange feels confrontational.

The fellow asks what my understanding and experience is. He then proceeds to tell me how to practice, pointing out the error of my ways and possible pitfalls. It would serve me best to put into practice something one of my teachers once shared: a Japanese response of smile, nod, and "perhaps you are right" to provide the fellow with the approval he seeks and allow me a gentle end to the discussion. But I keep on, finding clever ways to defend my practices and show him the rigidity of his views. As the fellow shares his beliefs about Buddhism, I can't help but feel repulsed—the opposite of the love I feel for Buddhism as the Rinpoche shares the teachings. A retort comes to mind. I am quick to share it with the fellow who continues to recline over the back of his chair.

"I am reminded of a quote by Gandhi," I say. "Something about...I like your Jesus. How come your Christians are so unlike your Jesus?" I think he might get the hint, though it comes out as more of a sting.

"You have to pick one path," he continues. "You can't just sample them all."

"Do you not believe that all paths hold the same seed at their root?" I ask, feeling the heat fill my cheeks. "That it is only in the processes that we see the difference?"

"You pick one way and endure it," he stated.

A laugh surfaces to soothe my flushed face while his words touch a truth inside me, which I happily share with him. "My intention has never been to endure it, but to enjoy it," I reply.

I enjoyed sampling all the various traditions, even more so, loved to watch those participating in their traditions and witness how in love they are with their beautiful practices. Perhaps all the various ways may be confusing to my mind at times, but observing people in love with their traditions fills my heart and connects me with many people, enhancing my compassion and joy for others.

My conversation with the fellow reminds me to be a careful teacher myself. When I share my words with others, I must also speak and write carefully, speaking only about that which I know. This is why I write memoir. After all, all I really know about is my experiences—and what they reveal to me. It does not mean I am opposed to the teachings of others. On the contrary. I only need to investigate how those teachings can be put into practice in my life.

It seems the fellow's intention is to convince this young girl— me—of no formal spiritual training, who spoke of receiving most of her guidance through meditation, that she needs to follow a teacher. Granted, a weird sensation arises: a deep-seated gender conditioning that has me wanting to comply to this outspoken fellow. Like a play set in ancient times on a worn stage, I'm like a character who has been type-cast in only one role and the exchange with my fellow actor is of lines deeply etched in stone an eternity ago. I am amazed to witness a pattern so entrenched.

The fellow calls me cynical, twice, to explain how I am unable to pick only one teaching. I've never been called cynical, ever, and I've been called a lot of things, so the word pokes me like a hot needle.

I take my seat as the Rinpoche enters the room for the final lecture of the session. I no longer enjoy the contentment and ease I had during the previous lectures. I'm disturbed by my conversation with the fellow. I'm agitated, and I recognize that agitation.

Often, during my spiritual seeking, a time comes toward the end of the practice that shines a light on the teachings and forces me to take a hard look at what I truly feel and believe about the experience. Some event occurs to push me into discomfort with the material: like a test. It used to upset me when it happened. I initially assumed I was in the wrong place, wrongly seeking or too immature spiritually to understand the material. I'd come to recognize this pattern, however, and I suddenly understood the purpose of the upset I felt in my unexpected exchange with the fellow.

I knew the encounter forced me to contemplate what I'd just learned. It was like a Dharma test from *The Way of the Bodhisattva*, to see if:

A) I am attentive to the teachings and heard the Rinpoche's words,

B) I give thought to what I've heard and can assimilate it in my life, and

C) my motivations are pure—am I using the teachings to gain status, money, or for my pride, or do I use them for the benefit of all sentient beings?

Understanding the test doesn't stop me from feeling upset, but it does stop me from reeling out of control. I have the first two answers nailed. The third is a bit grey as I could easily make a spiritual pissing match my intention: to one-up the fellow and be holier than thou in my conduct. Let's face it, I was stumbling all over that line.

I focus on the Rinpoche's words and my steady breath. Then the Rinpoche begins to use a word he'd not used during the other lectures. Many times he speaks of the word *discernment*.

I write quickly as I see an opportunity to gain deeper understanding into the meaning of my essence for spring. While I jot away in my notebook, the fellow turns toward me, leaning over in his seat and points at my journal saying, "You can't write that down, you didn't get it from meditation."

Are you kidding me?! I'm not so much appalled with what he said to me, but that he did so as the Rinpoche was speaking to the group. For some reason, I'd gotten under this fellow's skin enough to distract him from hearing the words of a teacher his own community had brought to speak. Clearly, we were each other's teacher. Both with lessons to learn and work to do.

For that, I thanked him. Everyone we meet is a teacher in some way, showing us where we have work to do. It's not to judge their views as right or wrong, but to reflect our own views, our attachments to them, and from where we derive our wisdom. To see the conditions we all have in common.

In my notes, I record the Rinproche's words on discernment. He speaks of it akin to wisdom, using discernment to "illuminate afflictions like ignorance and confusion." It is more than higher choices, it is seeing the root of suffering so as not to be distracted by it. It is like the agitation that comes at the end of exploration for me. It serves to test my discernment. Can I see my own conditioning, my reason for seeking, my intention for the information, and how to practice the teachings in my own life should I deem them necessary? Do I recognize the conditioning and afflictions in another?

As the session wraps up, the fellow calls me over to offer a sort of apology, saying he didn't mean to be a "hard-ass" about things. Then he informs me, rather, warns me, that meditation alone, with no teacher, can get me into trouble.

He assumes I have neither been taught meditation nor

have a teacher. Somehow his apology gets lost in that warning. The fellow says there is no point in re-inventing the wheel when others have already shown us the way. *Forgive me, but didn't the Rinpoche explain twice a verse in The Way of the Bodhisattva that encourages us to "Examine my words as you would examine gold"?*

After thanking the Rinpoche and asking him to return to Calgary, I head out of the building. As I walk down the sidewalk in the spring breeze, dead leaves scattering about my feet, it occurrs to me: one man's cynicism is another woman's discernment.

9

CONJURING TARA

MARCH 30TH, 2013

Om Tare Tuttare Ture Soha. I connect with Buddhist Goddess Tara on the front step. As I chant, a large bird sounds in the distance. Its call is prehistoric, hinting to its size. It sounds like a seagull but much much bigger. It flies directly overhead.

It is high yet still looms large, the size of an eagle. It is white or greyish in colour. It is not a seagull yet sounds similar. The wings are substantial and more square at the ends. An ocean of cloud drifts along nearby, like the wavy pattern of a sandbar.

A large cloud angel follows the bird's path. The cloud angel has wings spread wide and a long tail trailing across the sky. A cloud rainbow emerges and a glistening sundog arrives to sit next to it. *Om Tare Tuttare Ture Soha.*

10

ASK BIGGER QUESTIONS

APRIL 2ND, 2013

I doubt Einstein asked questions about himself. *Oh me, poor me, what is my purpose? How can I get along better with so-and-so?*

I bet he asked questions like: How can energy be harnessed? How can energy be used to make life better for humanity?

I imagine Einstein had bigger questions than the average person, which led him to bigger discoveries than the average person.

What if we step outside of our own perceived drama and unwrap our minds from ourselves? How can we improve health? How can disease no longer exist? How can the oceans be restored to pristine state? How can all villages, cities and communities become vibrant places to work, live, grow and thrive? How can the entire planet's populations, including wildlife and plant life, live in harmony?

What if we started contemplating bigger questions?

How can happiness become the effortless and natural state of the world? How can all people have access to clean water? Great schools? Art? Nutritious food? Satisfying work? Health care? How can we all do this together?

I'd like to know what questions Einstein asked.

11

EVENING MEDITATION WITH LEO
PART 1

APRIL 4, 2013

We sit in a circle in the lower level of the house that Leo is house-sitting. A fireplace makes the room cozy and we light many candles on the table in the centre circle. Leo asks us to pair up and turn to face our partner. I take a seat by the fireplace next to a man I don't know. He is wearing a grey toque and I wondered if he is ill. He seems older but it is difficult to tell how old with his toque on.

"One partner goes into giving mode and thinks of a word while the other partner prepares to receive." Leo guides us into the exercise. "The word is not spoken aloud but focused upon with the mind. The partner then shares what they receive."

I receive a lot more than a word. I get a story. A motion picture unfolds in my mind. I see the man walking along the train tracks with a 'hobo' sack tied to a stick over his shoulder. I try to decipher what I see in order to make sense of it. I fear perhaps he is undergoing cancer treatment and this is a sign of him checking out. My mind assumes the image means the end of his life.

How do I share this with him? Don't. Not in front of this group. Not at all. Me, myself and I debate the approach in my head. *Do not tell this man that he is going to die. But that's what I saw. Is it? Did you actually see him dying? Well, no, but... Then don't say it.* I choose to simply share the image with him that I received.

"Oh, cool," he responds. "Yeah, I have to move from the house I live in and I wasn't sure where I'd go. I can't afford to stay in my neighbourhood, so I might have to start looking on the other side of the train tracks. It's not as nice as my current neighbourhood, but I guess I'll give it a try."

Whew. See? I told you to hold your tongue about the story your mind pieced together. In my desire to make sense of the images I received, I would have tainted the picture by placing my own interpretation upon it. I'd never been so grateful for the committee in my head.

12

EVENING MEDITATION WITH LEO PART 2

APRIL 4TH, 2013

Once everyone in the group shared their experience, Leo guides us through a meditation to meet a white buffalo calf. It is easy to travel on Leo's voice. Imagery becomes vivid and clear, messages become frequent. As I begin to slip into a meditative state, White Buffalo Calf Woman appears with a message for me.

"Show them another way," she says.

I am walking in a field. It is the same field as in the picture from last night's dream; long, dry grasses of late summer or early fall. Leo and I walk the railroad tracks set into the prairie field. I couldn't see them in my dream but I see them in the meditation.

We arrive near a village. I see teepees in the distance. Children run to greet us. Women approach, waving. I wave back. Men on horses with Elders standing behind them all greet us warmly. They place their left hands over their hearts asking me to do the same and speak only from the heart while with them.

They lead me to a medicine wheel in my honour. I sit between the male Shaman and Deer Medicine Woman. The male Elders are on my right and the women are on my left. We sit on long logs laid upon the grass.

The medicine man points off into the distance across from me. A white buffalo calf appears. Deer Medicine Woman takes my hand and lead me to the buffalo. She places my hand on the buffalo's head. "He is called Great Spirit." I lay with him, head to head.

I begin to cry. "I am afraid they will kill you," I wail. "That you and Mother Earth will be killed."

"I cannot be killed," he says. "You cannot be killed." As if he is I, and I am him. An enormous wave of grief rises from me and tears spill from my actual eyes during the meditation.

I focus on my breath, trying to steady it and return to the white buffalo. *I hear his words but they don't bring me comfort: as if I am scared that no one believes anymore, and that lack of belief is killing Spirit and the spirit in me. I stay with him. I kiss and hug him, "Thank you," I whisper. "I love you."*

Deer Medicine Woman takes me from the ground and hugs me. She then lead me back to the circle. I sit on the log and she offers me herbal tea.

"Drink it," she says. "It will comfort you."

I feel as though I am meant to pass this comfort on to others.

"Will you help me?" I ask her.

"Yes," she says.

It is time to go. A child collects my cup and I hug her. Then I walk with Deer Medicine Woman to the edge of the village. I hug her goodbye and thank her. I thank the tribe as they wave goodbye to me. I feel loved and safe with the tribe: happy and included and deeply honoured to sit among the Elders and between the Shaman and Medicine Woman.

As Leo begins to pull the group from the meditation, I quickly wipe tears from my eyes. The room is thick with silence and lingering Spirit. No one speaks. I pull my journal from my bag next to my chair and write:

Deer medicine is family medicine: gentle and nurturing.

Hold the faces of your loved ones. Look into their eyes when speaking. Ask them how they are.

13

THE FIRST APPLE

MAY 20TH, 2014

Early morning on the mountain in the trees. I find a place to sit with a view of the sun rising on the Rocky Mountains. I eat my apple. Today is our apple fast. Three apples, one for each meal, during this final full day of our Qigong retreat. Before my first bite, I smell the apple and listen to it. When I hold it to my ear, I hear its lineage. I know its seeds go back to the first apple and it contains the blueprint. In that moment, I know that I, too, contain the seeds of the first human.

> "Take the Universe as your playmate and then see what happens."
>
> — ~JEAN HOUSTON

PART II
THE TWO ALBERTS

14

A MATTER OF ENERGY

SEPTEMBER 28TH, 2014

"Be who you are. Know who you are." I hear the words spoken by Master Jesus.

Months earlier in meditation, I had lined up the Masters and asked whoever was best-suited to work with me at the time to step forward. I believe I'd had my eye on Mother Mary or perhaps Master Buddha. I was surprised when Master Jesus had stepped up. I guess I was still reconciling his appearance in my life at the chapel in Sedona.

Who am I? I respond.

"You need to know who you are and gain insight *your* way, not merely follow the practices of others."

I think about what interests me, what I have a burning desire to understand: Energy.

So, as Jean Houston taught me, described in *Awakening on Purpose: Trusting the call*, I ask the Master of Energy to come forward and teach me everything there is to know about energy: its nature, its source, and how to work with it.

Immediately, Albert Einstein comes to mind and appears before me. He sits down on the step to my right.

Then another Albert appears. Albert Schweitzer. I don't know anything about him. *What fun!* He sits to my left.

Together, they show me the movement of energy. That which has form moves slower. The denser the form, the slower the movement. The formless moves quickly. Energy crashes into (rather, attracts) other energy to create form. They show me that is what astral travel is about. Time-travel is possible because of this nature of energy. We cannot travel in our physical bodies; they are too dense and slow, held by time. However, our thoughts are formless, our consciousness is formless; we can travel this way because formless moves fast. We can visit other times, dimensions, *realities* by time-traveling through our consciousness: thoughts and the formless parts of us.

The two Alberts tell me that I can work each day with them to learn more. I consider stopping there to absorb what they have shown me. Simple and powerful. But I want to know more. I ask about light energy. "How does coloured light work?"

"We use it for healing organs." They show me light energy – white energy passing through form energy becomes coloured. The form may be very light in density – a gas – but it is still form. It was harder for me to hold my focus on the light lesson.

They show me Newton's First Law of Motion: how objects in motion remain in motion unless acted upon by an outside force. They show me how the Big Bang or initial burst of energy put objects in motion and the formed objects must live out their nature. We are not able to stop the motion of the formed. Other forms will bump the formed around, but it is the nature of the formed to continuous motion.

As the formed continues to move outward, collectively

we can draw the formless back to itself. *What does this mean? A reassembly of source energy? A still point? A detachment from the formed?*

Mental exhaustion meets with physical exhilaration and our lesson completes. I say goodbye to the two Alberts. They walk off, arms around each other's shoulders: good friends. When I say goodbye to Master Jesus, he leaves me with this:

> "Follow your interests, let them lead you to the discoveries you are to make in this life."

LESSON 2
SEPTEMBER 29TH, 2014

I wasn't going to call in the two Alberts this morning, but a little way into my meditation, they arrived.

They show me my husband, Steve, biking down the path to work and going fast, then applying his brake: object in motion/outside force. Objects of form in motion effect other objects of form in motion more directly, whereas the subtle (formless) energies effect the subtle energies more directly.

"It takes a greater concentration of the formless to effect a change on the formed."

This is to say, it takes greater meditative/mental/emotional concentration to affect the physical. Which means either one person engaged in great concentration, or many people focusing the subtle energies.

If all beings on earth focus their attention/intention (subtle energies) on one desire/thought/emotion (say, love or healing), how would this affect the formed?

As I mentally repeat, *it takes a greater concentration of the formless to effect a change on the formed*, two ravens flap overhead, signalling the end of lesson two. I thank the two Alberts.

16

SHORT AND POWERFUL LESSON

SEPTEMBER 30TH, 2014

Use those of the formless to concentrate the energy.

By taking on the energy of the Masters – Buddha, Jesus, Kwan Yin, or Chenrezig, we can concentrate the energy of the formless more quickly and use it to effect the formed.

Master Lin teaches merging your energy with that of your Master's. This is employing the two Alberts' principle. Prayer, then, can become powerful when joined with those energies in the *formless*: Masters, Wisdom Beings, Angels, those who have passed and know how to wield their formless shape – pointed at a single focus.

Connecting with the energy of the Ancestors, Masters, Wisdom Beings and Angels essentially concentrates the formless exponentially more than we can ever do alone: learning to harvest the formless and focus that energy to effect change on an object.

LESSON 4
OCTOBER 1ST, 2014

It's fun having them come every day. The sky is clear and the stars are bright. Orion and the gang greet me in the dark of early morning.

The two Alberts show me my busy brain and how hard it can be to keep errant thoughts out. My heart centre is warm from focusing the first part of my meditation on opening it more.

They show me how the brain is busy because thoughts have been allowed to gain great concentration over the years. Strengthen the concentration of subtle energy in the heart and it will be stronger than the thought energy. Spend more time focused on the heart and less on the thoughts. Same with lower dantien: the qigong energy point behind the naval. Concentrated heart energy sends signals of well-being to the body: love, joy, peacefulness, thankfulness, contentment – like Master Lin spoke of.

A rabbit runs by. The two Alberts show me how this is true of fear energy *and* love energy – you can increase the concentration of either. It's all about concentration of energy. *Enough concentration of formless energy comes into form.*

As I repeat this concept, fog passes by the streetlamp. Water and air are sensitive to formless energy. They are closest to it, therefore they become vehicles for formless to concentrate into the formed, having a more direct effect on other forms.

Always bless your water.

18

JESUS & THE TWO ALBERTS

OCTOBER 2ND, 2014

We've got it a bit backwards – because we live in form, we forget we are formless beings too, and that's the part of us that is eternal: the subtle energy that continues on.

Lesson: *the formed affects the formless quicker because of its density (concentration) of energy.*

Humming, dancing, singing, sound (variations of form): all affect the formless. Dance or hum and feel the energy move through your body. You don't require as much effort since the singing has form – higher concentration – density of energy.

Likewise, food energy affects the subtle body. What we eat impacts our formless systems.

Next time you are on the giving or receiving end of a great hug, feel how that hug (form) affects your subtle energy (formless). Do you tingle from head to toe? Do you suddenly feel happy? Relieved? Comforted?

In our formed state (human bodies) we can impact the formless. It's all just energy.

LESSON 6
OCTOBER 3RD, 2014

This morning's lesson is an experience. The sun is coming up and I feel the first rays – my subtle body responds – lovely tingling, opening of channels, lightness of being, happiness.

The two Alberts show me how concentrated the sun's energy is, often too concentrated for our form. This concentration of formless energy impacts our form often too strongly at its peak– midday.

However, sunrise and sunset are filtered sunlight– the concentration is enough to effect change on our subtle/formless energy but not enough to change the formed: tan, burn, dry etc.The moon is another type of filter for the sun's energy. The reflected light is easy to take and effects only our formless energy: moon bathing.

I contemplate this lesson and thank the two Alberts.

Later, at tea, I remember the Pope who had died of a heart attack thirty-three days into his papacy: Pope John Paul I. I remember thinking how he had suddenly received too much love at once – from all the people. Too high of a concentration of energy for his heart centre.

This shows me the importance of using a filter to affect the subtle body and not forcing too high a concentration of energy at any particular form.

I consider my own spinal injuries and kundalini awakening. Master Lin once said that kundalini energy rising can be too powerful, too explosive for someone who has injury or illness. I think about my own spine, my discs being disrupted by the sudden influx of energy.

20

FREQUENT FREQUENCY

OCTOBER 4TH, 2014

Today's lesson is about energy concentration and frequency.

If something is low-frequency and you add a greater concentration of high frequency to it, the high frequency becomes the dominant frequency. This is true in the body and on the planet.

Again, following yesterday's lesson, if the concentration is high, it affects the formed - the tissues and cells - if it's not too concentrated, then only the subtle body is affected.

If I smile and have a nice thought, it makes my body tingle, and I feel lighter and relaxed: a concentration of higher frequency energy. When the early morning sun's rays shine on my face, even more tingling than my happy thought occurs: higher concentration yet of higher frequency.

I ponder if mixing lower and higher frequencies is like a chemical reaction: would they create new frequencies?

When I first visited Sedona, I couldn't sleep. A low hum reverberated my ears. I realized that it was the frequency of Sedona. Back in Calgary, I have a constant high-pitched whine in my ears at meditation and bedtime: the frequency of the city drowns out the frequency of Earth. Cell towers, electrical poles and boxes, street lamps... all of these emit frequencies. Our body is naturally attuned to Earth. Low concentrations of these frequencies affect the subtly body. High concentrations, however, affect the form.

Which begs the question: **Can I hold a vibration of harmony or health in the midst of bombardment of artificial frequencies?** I contemplate the lesson post-meditation...

Think about an angry mob. High concentration of a certain frequency. Now think about one million meditators. High concentration of a different frequency.

Now think about Sedona's low hum. A day or two and not much changes. After a few days, however, maybe the cells responding to the hum bring other cells into that frequency.

Now think about the city. A couple days, no difference. A week in the concentrated higher frequencies and fast-moving cells bring other cells up to their frequency: a frequency not designed for harmony or ideal health.

LESSON 8
OCTOBER 5TH, 2014

Today's lesson is about emotions.

The higher the concentration, the greater the affect on the body – formless affecting form. The lower the frequency, the denser (and slower) the object. The higher the frequency, the lighter (and quicker) the object.

High concentration of emotion (low vibration like fear) for a prolonged period of time = an effect on form = to vibrational frequency of emotion (slow and dense). Similar to cortisol - over a prolonged period, cortisol weighs on the immune system, suppressing it.

Now, equally, high vibrational emotions (quick and light like joy) in enough concentration, affect low vibration emotions. As we learned yesterday, a higher concentration of high frequency will surpass a lower concentration of another frequency.

This is a good case for happiness: if you feel sad and lonely for a prolonged period, these lower vibrations, in high concentration, will affect form and in fact may manifest form – like a tumor?

However, feeling happiness, contentment, joy, light-heartedness more often in higher concentration, will become the dominant frequency.

I ask about how certain emotions affect certain organs – the answer appears to be that emotions don't come from the brain but the energetic field of the organs themselves.

Or: the frequency of the emotion is similar wavelength to that organ's signals.

As I make my tea later in the day, I see how this is true for the frequency of food as well. Higher frequency foods provide high frequency energy to the body. Low frequency foods provide low frequency energy to the body.

Too much of a good thing:

This explains why, when we take a lot of a high concentration of energy– even high-frequency– it affects the form. Too much lavender can cause headache. A little can remedy it. A little chocolate increases dopamine, too much suppresses it. This is especially true with herbal remedies that have already increased the concentration of the herb: tinctures, essential oils, etc.

Formless affects formless– keep the subtle body energy clear and flowing– the formed body has intelligent processes to maintain itself. When the burden of heavy energy is too high, increase the higher frequency energy.

This is also true of words and thoughts:

higher frequency– light

lower frequency– dense

Keep the energy light and moving in order to avoid stagnant energy and blockages.

The ego is forever working to harness and control energy–
when the goal is really to understand its nature.
(the nature of energy)

PART III

TWO WORLDS WOVEN TOGETHER

22

CRISIS TO CREATIVITY
OCTOBER 21ST, 2014

My back blew two days ago after an awesome workout at the YMCA. I was hauling in all of the groceries and decided to go to the front door rather than to the garage. I bent over to ring the doorbell with my chin and when I stood up: compression, pain and loss of legs.

I am sitting in acceptance of it and deep contemplation while mitigating the pain with nervines – strange, as I recently picked up chamomile, thinking how I needed to take care of my nerves. Perhaps I was eavesdropping on my nervous system.

Last night, I had many hot flashes– a side effect from the spinal injury– kundalini energy on the move. I tried to move the energy, shift it myself.

Master Lin, at level 4 Spring Forest Qigong™ retreat, mentioned that if kundalini energy travels the wrong path, it damages the nervous system. It occurred to me at the time that perhaps that's what happened to me during my initial injury eleven years ago. I didn't even know about kundalini then.

In the middle of the night, during a hot flash, I think perhaps I should email Master Lin and ask him about how to get the energy on the right track. I look him up on Facebook the next day but his messaging is disabled– smart move, I think.

I decide to reach him the way he had taught us: through meditation. This will take my seeking from my mind's need for answers to a more holistic response as I receive information through more channels than the mental one.

I calm my body and mind, and then invite Master Lin to connect with me. He comes and sits in the chair next to me. I start crying. I don't know why. Crying always seems to precipitate healing for me. All sorts of stuff bubbles up. The space between my eyebrows hurts and I feel immense pressure. "I'm angry," I say. "Angry that there is so much suffering in the world and making peace with myself doesn't make any of it any better."

I tell him a bit about my injury and his inference in level 4 to kundalini energy. Pain strikes the back of my left shoulder. Master Lin stands behind me and pulls down on my shoulders. "Let it come," he says.

I ask him my question. "How can I get the kundalini energy on the right track?"

"Blockages are being cleared by the kundalini energy. When you were in bed for thirty-three days with this injury, many blockages were cleared." He continues, "The body knows what it is doing. Your soul knows what it is doing. Let it do its work."

I suddenly understand how people succumb to their illness. It is not a giving up but rather a surrendering to the growth and healing their soul came here for. Master Lin works for a moment or two on my back, then I thank him, and we say our goodbyes. I sit quietly for a few moments after the meditation and receive an insight.

The earth is a sacred place, like a hot spring or a cave. Beings from all over the cosmos come here to heal. Only we forget and get in the way. We were never meant to stay so long– like most sacred sites: you come for a reason and leave. We need to restore this sacred site since we are damaging her, trying to get something we can't remember. Trying to stay too long.

We are visitors and need to understand the nature of our injuries, wounds, or reasons to come here. We can also seek to understand why others around us have come. Each of us is visiting this sacred site in order to heal or learn something. We must be quiet and still in order to understand and allow the process to unfold.

23

ALL THE FIXINGS

OCTOBER 29TH, 2014

All these years of seeking is just now giving way to deep surrender. I no longer have the need to be anyone's teacher. I've been trying to be the source of everything for others: the source of strength, insight, wisdom.

I feel like I can't help anyone. Not in the way I want. I have to let people help themselves, or not. I feel ready to stop needing to be the source of anything for anyone. I feel ready to simply be at peace with me and life and the unknown story of who we are, where we came from and why we are here. Why all the fuss?

The lesson this season has been: Can I be present with the suffering of another without having to save them? Allow my daughter to have a cold without having to heal her? Allow my back to ache, the discs to bulge and impinge the nerves without carrying the burden of having to heal them?

It was a speedy recovery this week from my back pain. Last Sunday I could barely stand on my own – my husband decompressed me several times, carrying me over his back around the house – to doing gentle yoga a week later and walking to my son's school to pick him up.

I am learning to stop needing to fix everything. I'm learning to simply stay with things, allow them to be as they are, giving only my kind attention, peacefulness and love.

24

HALLOWEEN DREAMS
OCTOBER 31ST, 2014

I go to one of my favourite stores, like a Patagonia or Mountain Equipment Co-op. I can't remember the name. They have been advertising three stages for years – like red, white and blue or something. They have added silver, gold and platinum, and have become very forward thinking. Their owner is also a masterfully spiritual person.

I am in the store with two people, two friends, reading books and looking at merchandise in the store. Suddenly, he is there: the owner. We get to talk to him. He shows me his signature Buddha move. He waves his hand in the air and many small circles of smoke appear. Then he waves them again in the smoke and a perfect Buddha appears.

I'm so happy to be able to see it, faint in the smoke. I can see Buddha's image.

The owner is humble, no ego. I feel fortunate to meet him, though I forget his name.

25

CHOP WOOD, CARRY WATER

My dear and long-time friend, Anna, spent two weeks at her daughter's school sharing yoga and gratitude with the students. She says it was well-received and shifted the school. She laughs as she tells me a story about her experience there.

She says there was a lice issue among the younger grades and each day she and the teachers had to scrub the yoga mats. Then she says something that reminds me very much of the old Zen saying: "Before enlightenment, chop wood, carry water. After enlightenment, chop wood, carry water."

> "You can open hearts, you can open minds, but you still have to scrub the mats." ~ Anna

26

SCOTTISH ANCESTORS

MAY 16TH, 2015

vision unfolds, more like a daydream. I pull on a thread and allow it to unravel.

A Scottish time traveller arrives here. He is confused as to where (when) he is. I investigate his lineage. He will be father or grandfather to a son I see in a vision from his dead father/uncle figure.

I see a gold crown: old, Scottish crown, very simple, very old. And I hear the name David. I'm not even sure that name would exist in old Scotland and consider changing it during my vision.

After the front step, I check Facebook posts. One of the teachers I follow has posted a photo of a white stag from Scotland, along with a tale of a most beloved King David I of Scotland, whose father was Malcolm Canmore.

Really? Canmore?

I lived in Canmore in my late twenties. The Rocky

Mountain town is a fifty-five-minute drive from my home. I look up the information and discover that the town of Canmore is indeed named for Canmore, Scotland: reigning King Malcolm III, David's dad.

Strange things are happening. Time is speaking to me.

27

NATURE'S STAG

JUNE 19TH, 2015

I pause along the path that circles the pond. *How do I help people to return to the magic of Nature?*

The response: Focus on the elements: earth, water, air and fire.

What I do for one, I do for the other. As I say this phrase in my head, I hear huffing and puffing behind me. I turn to see a strong young stag deer bounding toward me, his substantial antlers thick with velvet.

His mouth is open as if he has been running for a while. His high stepping allows him to cover ground quickly and he crosses the hillside, makes his way to my sacred place and disappears over the hill.

I'm left glued to the path in awe of the experience. The similarity to the stag energy in the Facebook post and the Scotland connection has me in instant contemplation. *Ancestors?*

. . .

Nature is the healer, so said my dream of two nights ago. *Nature heals everything.*

Teach people that what we do to Earth, we do to ourselves.
There's an urgency to this message.

28

SOLSTICE DREAM

JUNE 21ST, 2015

A large tree trunk
    evergreens
        a path

I see my bare feet – beautiful toes and white nightshirt hem. I run along the mossy green grassy path – Celtic.

misty air

emerald green forest

I come to a large rock: old friend. I climb up and sit. I remember all the times, all the rocks I have sat upon – from the tree-lined field rock at home on the farm to Cathedral Rock, Bell and Shnebly in Sedona, to the river rock while camping. All the rocks gift me healing and nourishing experiences. Purification – innocence.

I sit with the rock then take the flower wreath from my hair – white flowers – and place it on the rock as I leave – running back down the path, my feet, my hem. I kneel at the guardian tree and place a strand of my hair.

I've been here before.

29

FRONT STEP Q&A
JULY 27TH, 2015

I ask of the wisdom beings, "How can I hear you?" The kestrel glides low over the fence at me. They speak through nature. I ask my questions while the door of communication is open to them.

    Q: What does humanity need?
        A: To restore their faith.
    Q: Faith in what?
        A: Themselves.

30

WEAVING
AUGUST 9TH, 2015

Sitting on the front step with a friend. She points to a spider in a web behind me. The spider has woven one of my hairs into her web.

I am part of the fabric of life.

Woven into the universe itself.

We move together now.

PART IV
PERSPECTIVE

31

PICKING BONES

JANUARY 17TH, 2016

On the front step this morning, I have a heart-to-heart with Nature. I remember a time when I needed nothing from her, rather, I sought nothing from her. Simple enjoyment.

She is my beloved!

As I get ready to go back inside, I suddenly notice a sizeable bone, picked clean, on the ground next to the step. A chicken leg, perhaps, or rabbit. Bird tracks are near – *gift from Raven?*

The bone sends chills into my own – not the frightening kind of chills, but the kind that comes with unravelling a mystery – with the wisdom of our beginnings, our lives, our stories: our individual and collective stories.

So many bones
    so many buried
    so many secrets

so many keys
so many stories
so many lives
so many lifetimes.

I thank Raven, or whichever bird friend left me this gift, and I know to listen today because of this sign.

I return indoors to tea and email. I open the one from Upaya Zen Centre, celebrating a member of their Sangha: an author. Her book?

Writing Down the Bones: Freeing your Inner Writer by Natalie Goldberg

I'm listening
I'm sensing
I'm feeling into the flow
the guidance and wisdom of my story
my nature in rhythm with Nature.

32

DREAMTIME EAGLE

JANUARY 24TH, 2016

I am standing outside with someone – male – on a highway/walkway/bridge-type structure. There are many people on the grounds around us.

Suddenly, I see a large eagle. I notice a wing, just out of sight, and realize that there is a pair of eagles.

The large eagle descends directly in front of me. As he lands, I understand just how big he is – bigger than me! He is a bald eagle. I feel incredibly fortunate and proud that he has picked me: as if he is saying, "you are the one," in a sacred and powerful way.

I am also afraid, as I know his beak could shred my face. His great, golden beak is higher than the top of my head and when he lands, he stands on my feet, as if to keep me in place with him.

This is all I remember.

We are each great beings. We have simply forgotten this.

33

TAKE FLIGHT

FEBRUARY 5TH, 2016

I watch Magpie sail on the strong chinook winds, circling around to land on the neighbour's roof. Her tail seems fragile as it whips in the wind.

I fear for her seemingly fragile tail feathers – *could the wind whip them from her?*

Magpie doesn't fear this. She navigates the wind with her senses, her instincts and her agility. She was born to fly.

>Don't use your conditioning (fears) to navigate.
>>Use your instincts.

THE SPIRAL
MARCH 29TH, 2016

Stop looking at life in a linear manner. It is a spiral.

I am contemplating the spiral – everything is available/happening NOW: past, present, future. What I'm writing is already written and also not yet in conception.

This time of deep rest is slowing me – my thoughts – mind-watching, sensing, feeling more.

There is loud banging outside. It is 7AM. I am annoyed in my meditation, annoyed with the noise. *How can I continue my contemplation with all of this noise?*

I remember that everything is an opportunity to practice: every thought, every emotion, conversation, encounter. In this spiral nothing is separate. Nothing is outside of me.

Then I become the sound of the banging and I am no longer annoyed.

35

SAME SHIT, DIFFERENT PILE

APRIL 14TH, 2016

I seek spiritual practices – yoga, Buddhism, meditation – to settle a mind that is busy striving for perfectionism: setting the bar, achieving.

Then I realize the mind has only shifted its focus and is still driving for perfect practice, perfect mind, perfect meditation: more struggle.

And I let it **all** go

and fall back into life.

"The feeling of being hurried is not usually the result of living a full life and having no time. It is on the contrary born of a vague fear that we are wasting our life."

— ERIC HOFFER

36

THE ROSE MEDITATION
APRIL 25TH, 2016

I drop into meditation, inviting Tara to help me open my heart. I move the ball of light from my lower dantien to my heart (as Master Chunyi Lin has taught me), smile on my face, surrounded by light, all channels in my body opening.

As I remain in the light with Tara (hearing the rain fall and the birds sing), I move my breath to my heart – inhaling, feeling my heart centre warm, then exhaling.

Tara gifts me the rose meditation. I envision a beautiful red rose in my heart – drops of dew on lush petals. Each time I inhale, I nourish the rose. Each exhale sends her fragrance out into the world. I begin to cry.

"I just want to help and heal everyone, the animals and Earth," I tell her.

"Of course you do," she replies, "because that's the way of the Bhodhisattva, but it gets confused in human life. Stop carrying the grief of the world."

She continues, "The way you can be of most benefit is to show up wherever you are with joy and love. Bring joy to others, to the land, your family."

This makes me infinitely happy.

37

FEEDING MY DEMONS

MAY 15TH, 2016

I am in forgiveness practice of the men in my life and the masculine. I put them all together into one being – one man to forgive.

Then I realize how much pain and suffering man (men) has inflicted: on Earth, Nature and women.

And I see all of the feminine needing to forgive all of the masculine. I put Lama Tsultrim Allione's teachings from her book *Feeding Your Demons* into practice and I feed this *man*. The food has the quality of love.

The man turns into a little boy and then a stuffed animal remains – teddy bear? It is snatched up quickly by Alice in Wonderland, who sits on the big chair in her blue dress with white apron and blonde hair. She says she is the ally – with her fast-talking-can't-get-a-word-in-edgewise way.

She says we will go on many marvellous adventures. Alice tells me that I can access her through tea – of course, silly.

Look at the world through a new lens.

A RING OF WISDOM

MAY 17TH, 2016

I bike around the community, when the teepee ring calls me in –

"Come to the medicine wheel, there you will heal."

I walk my bike down into the coulee and enter the teepee ring from the north. Red ants. *Great.*

I stand on the centre rock, deciding which direction has fewer ants. The south rock is partly covered by an overhanging Wolf Willow branch, but no red ants. I sit in the south.

"Great Spirit," I say, and then I start to cry. "I'm tired of the size of my pain body. I'm afraid of letting go of healing my spine and my pain; that if I let go of healing myself, I condemn myself to pain and suffering." But I want to let go of the expectation and constant drive to have to heal myself.

"I hate the hot flashes." There. I said it. In the teepee ring, aloud. I said it. And Spirit tells me to make them anything I wish. Choose what the hot flashes mean.

I laugh through my tears. I understand what Spirit means and it's kind of funny.

"Okay," I say, "when I have a hot flash it makes me younger… look younger, feel younger." I smile. "My hot flashes make me more beautiful, healthier, happier and funnier."

It's another perspective shift.

Spirit is telling me to make my life what I want. Choose what it means to me. I continue, "My head is busy all the time."

Spirit says don't think, FEEL. I thank Spirit and the teepee ring for my family and friends and the sacred land upon which I've lived and has held me and my family for over ten years.

"I've lived a blessed life. I am living a blessed life."

The wind through the trees applauds and cheers. I leave the teepee ring.

Choose what you want.

There is no agenda.

39

NATURE SHIFTS

MAY 18TH, 2016

Why is it that winter months feel so long and spring flies?

At the end of Jean Houston's course, she recommended *The Daily Optimist* online news in order to shift our perspective on the world's state.

The *Daily Optimist* is solutions journalism, and I'm surprised how, after reading about them and skimming their content, I *do* feel more optimistic about the world. I realize that they are right. "There aren't enough problems for all our solutions."

This shift in thinking and seeing, through their vast library of articles, helps me feel hopeful instead of hopeless. I had slowly been resigning myself and the planet to an inevitable end at the hand of man and resenting humanity for it.

I have begun the shift towards humanity working in tandem with Nature to evolve and elevate life on earth: in harmony with Nature.

The Fort McMurray fires evacuated the town of 88,000

people last week, burned 1600 structures and continues to consume boreal forest every day. My heart sinks for the people but even more for the loss of forest and animals.

A *Daily Optimist* article entitled "Young Forest... Carbon Capture" makes me realize Nature is one smart cookie. She is adapting, sacrificing parts of her, to capture more carbon.

We need to come on board and help in any way we can.

We are in this together. What we do for us, we do for Nature.

What we do for her, we do for us.

40

POST-FRONT STEP INSIGHT

MAY 22ND, 2016

I am reading Shiva Rae's *Tending the Heart Fire* (a gift from Anna), and it occurs to me...

In Ayurveda, *vata* is queen of the doshas. If you don't know which dosha to balance, you go to vata - once balanced, she pulls the other doshas into balance.

Perhaps, likewise, the heart chakra is queen of the chakras. If you don't know which chakra to address, go to the heart chakra, she will pull the others into balance.

> If you only do one practice for the rest of your life, forgiveness will be enough.

41

THE SILENCE

JUNE 9TH, 2016

I just dissolved my company.

"I closed the bank account, closed the GST account. I need to pay the accountant. Anything else I need to do?"

My husband is standing ten feet away, leaning against the kitchen counter, texting. He doesn't respond. I surf through PayPal pages, trying to remember if I closed that account.

"Check out this new golf shirt," he says, pulling it over his head. "Does it fit me okay? Oh, and I invited my sister and her kids to stay with us sometime in the next couple weeks," he continues, checking his shirt in the mirror.

"Our kids still have school," I reply. "and the deck is scheduled to get done sometime in the next couple weeks. I'm teaching class and start my spine rehab."

June is the busiest month. My dear friend and I always say, "Don't book anything in June." It's crazy: year-end school stuff fills the month.

June and September. Don't book anything. Also the nicest weather months.

"See you," he heads out the garage door for golf, leaving me to get the kids to sleep.

I follow him out to the driveway, along with my rage, and inform him of what I think about his texting while I talk, and his planning without consulting me.

I head back inside, slamming the garage door.

It's finally cool enough for sleep, after four straight days in the low 30s Celsius. The breeze through the kitchen window cools my feet and my mood.

I'm mad. I'm sad. Maybe, like that Pixar movie, I'm sad-mad. I talk my way around it, blaming him not consulting me, bringing in my lack of purpose or direction of work, self, hobbies. When you're triggered, everything comes into question; it's a free-for-all on why life sucks.

The whole week, month, year could have been spectacular, but in that one low moment, everything is shit.

I remember last night's dream. *I am on a roller coaster ride but not really. It's more like a ski lift: high, very high, over a city or amusement park. I am holding my daughter tightly in front of me. There is no safety bar. My husband is next to me and my son is squished between us. Why is there no safety bar?! I am holding my daughter for dear life trying to keep her safe.*

Why is there no safety bar?!

Back in waking life...

I crawl into bed next to my daughter to read a chapter of my book. My husband told her she could sleep in our bed since he will be home late for hockey: that always meant he slept downstairs so as not to wake me.

I mark my chapter with the flyer from the massage place. I remember my conversation with my friend earlier today. She was bothered by her mom's pending visit. She loves her mom. They have great times together.

She realized why she was bothered. It was June, and the last days to ourselves, kids and school. She wasn't ready to give up her remaining days of quiet reflection, simple solitude, personal space. Even if it was for her mom.

That's what triggered me. It wasn't my husband's texting or not consulting me before inviting his sister to stay. It was the final days of mom-freedom. My coveted time: to write, to sit on the deck, to not parent or prepare midday meals for others.

> I wasn't ready to relinquish the silence.

42

FOCUS
JUNE 9TH, 2016

That night, Nature enters my dreams. As I sleep just beneath the waves of waking life, wind knocks at my front door. *I open it and let them in.*

Standing in my living room, one man says, "He is here." Another man stands in my kitchen: a serious, First Nations man with the energy and physique of a strong warrior – not an Elder, but an important person in the tribe – a spokesman.

We sit on the front step. "Now is the time to focus," he says. I feel a return of the 'stop seeking' lesson I'd learned from Buddha during my forty-day practice: knowing source so we don't need to seek it. "Stop doubting," he continues. "You have all you need for what you are doing and are about to do."

"Focus. No more wasted energy on doubt or uncertainty. Show up. Keep showing up. Focus on your studies and your practices. They are important for what you do. Focus."

"Keep your thoughts and speech right. Focus. Do the work... words, actions, thoughts throughout each day. Focus.

"No doubt. You are exactly where you are meant to be. Deer Medicine Woman loves you. She is helping you with plant medicine."

He is more stern than the guides who usually come to me; he has serious work. "There is strength in focus. Don't waste it on doubt."

PART V
THE WAY FORWARD

43

DEATH IS TIRED

SEPTEMBER 14TH, 2017

I complete my Lojong practice (a form of Buddhist mind training).

I am listening to the sound of rain.
Breathing rain.

My mind moves to Waterton Park – areas of forests on fire. *I see the burned earth but the fires are out– rain.*
> *then Tara*
> *spreading golden light – nectar*
> > *a balm*
> *I chant the Lotus Pinnacle of Amoghapasha.*

> *To help the animals*

The grim reaper comes and sits on my left, the Angel of Death on my right. I haven't seen them in a long time, not since my encounter with them at the end of An Accidental Awakening. I laugh as I repeat the mantra, surprised yet happy to see them.

. . .

He's tired, the Grim Reaper. It's time for all sentient beings to move to higher realms. I keep repeating the short mantra for the bears, the squirrels, the moths and insects.

Om Padmo Ushnisha Vimale Hum Phat
Om Padmo Ushnisha Vimale Hum Phat
Om Padmo Ushnisha Vimale Hum Phat

44

MORE SHIFTING

NOVEMBER 19TH, 2017

The first kundalini energy blast (my low back) led to my first awakening: my year in yoga: big, bold, massive shifts.

The second (neck injury) was painful yet more of a subtle awakening in that I had to deal with life as it is.

The first was almost an escape... everything so big, fresh, new, magical... it was easy to get caught up in the alternating waves of curiosity and elation.

The second was: here comes a wave of anger. Can you sit with it? Can you befriend it? Here comes grief. Can you dissolve through it yet be present at the dinner table?

The first led me to thinking I could transcend my life, live a new life in a new way.

The second taught me that realization comes quietly, as you are, through the rising and falling of emotions as frequently as breath itself.

. . .

When despair for the world grows in me and I wake in the night at the least sound in fear of what my life and my children's lives may be, I go and lie down where the wood drake rests in his beauty on the water, and the great heron feeds. I come into the peace of wild things who do not tax their lives with forethought of grief. I come into the presence of still water... For a time I rest in the grace of the world, and am free.

— Wendell Berry, *The Peace of Wild Things*

45

FEEDING THE CORONAVIRUS DEMON

MARCH 15TH, 2020

It is early in Canada's Coronavirus plan. Schools are just now announcing closures.

Lama Tsultrim Allione offers an online *Feeding Your Demons* meditation session. I catch the tail end of it. Lama guides us through feeding the COVID-19 demon. I drop easily into the practice, even though it's been years since I've last fed a demon. This one is angry. The angriest demon I've met.

I recognize it immediately as a hydra demon: having many heads, many issues. It screams at me when I ask what it wants. I don't even think I finished my question.

"Respect me!!"

The demon has surfaced from Earth and her animals. It is Nature in angry form. As I begin to feed the demon, its heads spin wildly around like a ride at the Calgary Stampede. It consumes much nectar.

The demon slowly transforms into what I will soon know as the ally. A fat brown mouse sits in the chair in the demon's place. He is eating cake. His belly is round, and he is in no hurry to do anything other than enjoy his snack.

"How will you help me?" I ask him. I see the many tunnels and trails the mice have carved through the snow across my lawn during the winter: so many ways to get nourishment.

"Whatever you need, I can provide a path to it," he says.

There are over 1,000 of us live on Lama Tsultrim's online call. Each of our practices are done in silence, with only Lama speaking.

After practice, others comment on their experience. There is a shared essence of the demon. Taking on many forms – unique to each person – the demon wants the same thing: respect. We have violated his very nature. The very nature that provides all living beings with sustenance. We have disrespected our home.

My ally, mouse energy, the transformation of the demon, holds the wisdom to our continuation of life on planet Earth. Mouse will show us how to carve many paths forward.

DREAMTIME, GREENTIME
MARCH 27TH, 2020

I sit at a table with others.

The owner of our local superfood store is giving us a list of herbs to heal the coronavirus. I'm not writing them down like the others. I feel I have a good knowledge of herbs and am in good health.

My herbalist friend sits at the end of the table to my right. She knows all of what the store owner knows. She lays her head on her arms on the table.

I decide to write down the list of herbs, it will be good to have. I hear their names clearly, nothing I know well. I write down about three ...

Mrow

Mroooowwwww

My 21-year-old cat wakes me.

By the time I realize the importance of what I have dreamed, I can't grasp the names. They slip between my waking fingers back to Dreamtime.

Suddenly, a flash of waking dream floods my vision. Field of herbs. A warehouse/greenhouse of herbs. Instead of making masks to protect against coronavirus, they are growing herbs that heal/prevent it.

I'm disappointed that I can't remember the names of the herbs given to me in Dreamtime. I am, however, excited (hopeful) that the pathway is being forged.

All the herbs looked the same, like parsley or cilantro, though I know they weren't on the list.

Mouse is opening the way forward.

I head to the front steps to meditate. At the end of my meditation, I sit with Medicine Buddha. This time I dream an intentional dream. I envision fields of herbs, greenhouses, people's homes. We all cultivate the medicines. Farmers' markets offer a bounty of herbs alongside fruits and veggies. We all know how to eat for health and evolution.

I see the grocery stores: where meat once filled the shelves, now spills with deep green bundles of herbs.

47

LOVINGKINDNESS
MARCH 29TH, 2020

Last night, I dreamed that the Calgary Stampede, the Greatest Outdoor Show on Earth, was cancelled due to the virus.

While I feel sad for all the workers who will lose their jobs, I also feel the relief of the animals that were scheduled to perform for the masses. It is like a collective sigh and a softening.

While I have no idea whether the Stampede will proceed, I woke feeling as if Nature is getting a much-needed rest. Everything is so fast and demanding here on planet Earth. There was a sweetness to the feeling of the event not proceeding. This space of ease. Like the practice of *metta bhavana*, lovingkindness: letting everything off the hook. Slower. Simpler. Sweeter.

48

WORDS ON THE WIND DURING MY WALK

APRIL 3RD, 2020

Welcome, sister.

It might arrive as a lightning strike or it might sift through your dreams while you sleep. When it comes, you will wonder how you never knew it. But then you will remember that you've known it all along.

You will re-member your connection to all of life. A tremendous elation will arise. A great swelling of bliss will fill you. And then the other shoe will drop.

While you recover your relationship with Earth, you will also understand all of the suffering inflicted upon her. It will come as a crushing weight, as if you suddenly realize that your dearest love has been in pain for years and you've not noticed. Your heart will ache simultaneously with newfound love and newfound pain.

Once you lay waste to guilt and blame, you will grieve her. Hard. Do so. With every ounce of awareness, grieve her. Then make amends. Offer her your tears. Let them fall onto her soil, soak into her flesh. Apologize.

. . .

Dearest Mother,
I am sorry.
Please forgive me.
I love you.
And I thank you.

Then you'll get to work.

You'll do the holy work, the sacred work. You'll leave blessings in nature by way of writing poems in the snow and love letters in the sand. You'll chant the Heart Sutra to the forest and sing lullabies to the ocean. You'll hold a rock in both hands and squeeze every drop of gratitude you have into it before tucking it back into Earth's lap.

Then you'll do the practical work. You will live a simpler life. You will take what you need and use what you take. You will shrink your footprint. You will create beauty and celebrate nature. You will show others the way.

One step further... you will give back to Earth. You will plant both seeds of love and seeds of plants. You will reforest Earth and rewild her spaces. You will protect her animals. And you will be a great steward of her.

You will care for her as she has cared for you all along.
And you will notice how many of us are here with you doing this work.

Welcome, sister.

49

COYOTE MEDICINE

APRIL 23RD, 2021

I had no idea how life would change again for me. I thought I knew my new normal and that it would always be my normal: connected to the cosmic creative well, my meditations alive with meaning and magic.

What was woken through my lumbar spinal injury and my year in yoga during *An Accidental Awakening*, closed with my cervical spinal injury six years later. I didn't immediately realize the closure. My days were spent in pain management. The blissful states, the visions that once seemed effortless to slip into, stopped. Not only did it all end, but I was left in quite the physical state.

I desperately searched to regain the gifts I'd not realized were on loan to me. The Elder-woman. At my sacred place, I'd asked her for her gift of vision. I'd forgotten. Once I remembered, I could no longer be angry to have lost them, or upset with myself at a seemingly wrong turn I couldn't correct.

Once I remembered my request of the Elder-woman, I could only smile and bow and say thank you to her for the gifts that were not mine but I now know exist for each of us and all of us.

What lingers is the knowing. You can't scrub wisdom from your bones. I know what I know. I remember. I feel the energy alive around me and within. I trust. I lived lifetimes in those years.

And I return to life fully-immersed in this physical body, with all its aches and pains, and the awareness of what's beyond it yet contained in every cell. I continue to talk to the wind. I'm still more likely to pay attention to the birds than the person speaking to me. Who am I to judge what is meaningful or not in this life? Each of us lives our karma, our dharma and our dreams.

Be where your feet are. And know that there is so much more available to you. Extend your hand to Dreamtime. Better yet, extend your heart. Take the Cosmos as your dance partner. Sit with Wisdom Beings. Talk with sacred stones. Laugh with a single dandelion. Listen.

Be grateful everyday, for our time here is short.

"When you are inspired by some great purpose, some extraordinary project, all your thoughts break their bounds: Your mind transcends limitations, your consciousness expands in every direction and you find yourself in a new, great and wonderful world. Dormant forces, faculties and talents become alive, and you discover yourself to be a greater person by far than you ever dreamed yourself to be."

— Krishna Pattabhi Jois

JUICE YOUR DREAMS

We leave ourselves breadcrumbs to follow in this adventure called life on Earth. Sometimes we lose the trail or venture off on a side path. Meditate on your dream if you need further guidance and insight. Just know that the breadcrumb trail doesn't always reveal itself when you want it to.

Just because you searched for answers once and received little information doesn't mean if you search again later you won't find more. You can be certain you have hit a dead end only to later discover a wide open field.

This is why it is important to treat dreams as we do meditation: the point of meditation is to listen, observe, no-action. If we ask a question every night and try to process the information so we can act on it, we may find ourselves exhausted by this work.

Ask a question. Allow it to form over and over in Dreamtime. See it through many filters. Let it sit. Develop a relationship with your Dreamer and a recognition of your dream patterns. See the larger themes in your life.

I did not expect my dreams to become so responsive to my questions, especially early on. I could hardly keep up with the vast amount of information on a daily basis. By the time a year of dreaming was over, I needed a break. As I began the process of typing up my dreams, putting them into book form, I asked the Dreamer each night to gift me dreamless dreams. I asked for rest, rejuvenation, and regeneration during my sleep.

On the rare occasion I required direction, I would ask for a dream. Otherwise, I was spent from trying to process the sheer volume of information granted me in Dreamtime. Ask your question. Record your dream details. Juice the dream for more information, essence, representation, feelings. Make your notes and let it be.

Be patient. Build the relationship with your Dreamer and see the themes in your life. Understand the greater picture to see where inspired action is needed. Don't exhaust yourself on daily deciphering of Dreamtime.

Master Chunyi Lin mentioned that too much time spent in third eye depletes the energy and the physical body. Go to third eye when you need to but remember to then anchor your energy back into the body. I go to Dreamtime when I need to call upon it for insight or when it needs to call upon me. Each day, I return my energy to my lower dantien or anchor it into the lower chakras with Earth practices, yoga, Spring Forest Qigong, or intention.

To remain curious, to continue exploring for the sake of exploring, keeps the heart and mind young and the soul deeply satisfied. Be among children: instead of finding their antics silly, join in. Do what they do. They are following their curiosity. Use your wisdom to provide safe parameters but do not allow your fear to kill the curiosity. Expect no outcome.

What happens if I write what comes? With no expected

outcome. Without trying to figure out the ending or where the story is going. What if I let go of the need for it to take shape and simply follow it through its natural process?

What if I don't seek answers to my dreams but simply write them out, draw them out, for the fun of seeing them in daylight?

What if I follow things along – ideas, inspirations, dreams, meditations – just to see where they go? Pull the thread and unravel the cosmic blanket to see if there is something at the other end. Or not. Then go chase a grasshopper to see who's faster.

I don't want to know the answers to all my questions. I want to lay under the Christmas tree and enjoy the soft lights, the sappy scent, the sparkling tinsel and the magic of the holiday, like I did as a child. I want to smell the Scotch Pine and feel the prickly needles: see the tree from a new perspective. I want to taste the Christmas chocolates in fancy packaging beneath its boughs and participate in the full experience of the Christmas tree. Don't tell me the answers. Let me play.

Curiosity seeks nothing yet reveals everything in the moment.

I jot notes in my journal. There is a feeling of full circle. The cosmos gives form to the formless and somehow through writing, through putting my experiences, thoughts and life into words on the page, I return that energy back to the cosmos. Something is released when I crystallize my life on the page.

> "We are a way for the cosmos to know itself."
>
> — CARL SAGAN

YOUR TURN

The following pages are for you to record your experience with Dreamtime. You can also pick up your own journal. Start where you are, write what you can recall and deepen your connection to your Dreamer. It didn't always come easy for me. In fact, as you'll see in this excerpt from *Awakening on Purpose*, it once didn't come at all. And then it came all at once...

"Close your eyes," Alora cooed. "Notice anything flowing into your mind — ideas, judgments, thoughts — just notice as these same items flow out."

I allowed the movement of my mind to join my body.

"Renewal, release, rejuvenation," Alora suggested. "Any tension dissolving. Anything rigid, ideas or body, softening."

Each exhalation found within it a long, slow, audible sigh.

"Aaaaaahhhhhhhh," sighed Alora, "Letting go, letting flow."

"Aaaaaahhhhhhhh," the group echoed.

"Write down whatever wants to express itself through

your flowing practice ... images, words, thoughts or colours that surface while you move."

I imagined throwing down a couple drawings for show. I hadn't experienced the *visions* and *inner guidance* others in the group occasionally referred to. I also hadn't done much in the way of art since my teens, with the exception of preschool-style stickmen and smiley-faced suns drawn in crayon at the kitchen table with Michael and Khali.

As my body continued to expand and move in all directions throughout the yummy dog and cat poses, I noticed Yvonne reach for her crayons. Alluring and soft-spoken Yvonne walked with grace and dressed with seductive, creative flair. Her black cotton leggings revealed the flesh of her thighs beneath patterned lace. A flowing top draped over her pants as softly as her dark blonde, wavy hair draped over her face. I wondered at what point in my practice I needed to add a few stick men to my canvas.

I closed my eyes, returning to the wave of my breath and body. My hips rocked side to side and my head dropped toward the mat in surrender to the waves rolling up my spine. *Let go.* I encouraged my fear of pain to release its grip on my mind and muscles. Images emerged from nowhere. A large open eye, complete with long lashes, appeared in my *mind's eye*. A dolphin followed. Grey-blue iridescent skin sparkled as it crested the surface of the water. I forced my eyes open, wide in disbelief. I saw them, yet I didn't see them, not with my eyes anyway. I knew them, detailed in design yet vague in purpose, not a memory.

I dropped to my knees and tried to replicate the images on my canvas, making two attempts at the curve of the dolphin's back. I still saw it clearly in my mind but my hands couldn't reproduce the shape. I drew quickly, afraid the visions would fade as fast as they appeared.

I returned to the rhythm of the waves, surprised by how easily I slipped back into the flow. More visions surfaced, cresting the waters of my practice. I continued to draw, colour and record the spontaneous display in my head, swept away in the process.

There was more happening than yoga: a surreal experience, like an enchanting dream full of life and magic, yet I was a participant in this dream, recording its details and exploring its meaning as I explored movement in my body. It was as if, as I moved, ideas and images dislodged from my joints, memories broke free of my bones — released from their bodily cage, long held hostage. The sacred rhythmic union of body and breath aroused creativity.

DREAM JOURNAL

DREAM JOURNAL

DREAM JOURNAL

DREAM JOURNAL

DREAM JOURNAL

DREAM JOURNAL

DREAM JOURNAL

DREAM JOURNAL

Love to you,

Stephanie

IN GRATITUDE

Thank you, Maraya, for all the hours of feedback, editing and friendship.

Lama Tsultrim, for your wisdom and compassion, and for creating a space for the feminine in all her forms to flourish.

Levi, for sharing your way of living and seeing the world that let me know I wasn't crazy. And all the great bird conversations we have.

Master Lin, for your healing energy.

Family, friends and readers who love and support me no matter which path I walk that day. Or if I'm paying more attention to the birds than you.

I love you and I thank you.

ABOUT THE AUTHOR

Stephanie Hrehirchuk is a writer, spiritual seeker and teacher.

She is a multi-genre author who has a tree planted for every print copy sold of her Anna series of children's books.

Stephanie specializes in women's issues. She blogs, coaches and teaches about nutrition, health, yoga, meditation, the chakra system, the world of self-directed publishing, parenting/motherhood and spiritual pursuits.

She still drops the occasional f-bomb. She still hangs out with Anna. There is never a shortage of tea or dark chocolate.

ALSO BY STEPHANIE HREHIRCHUK

An Accidental Awakening: It's not about yoga; It's about family

Awakening on Purpose: Trusting the call

Nourish: Ayurveda-inspired 21-day Detox

Householder Yogini: Practices & journaling exercises for women who live at the intersection of spirituality & family

From Exercise to Ecstasy: 10 ways to turn body-mind into body-mind-spirit

Children's Books:

Anna and the Earth Angel

Anna and the Tree Fort

Anna and the Food Fort

Anna and the Christmas Tree

www.ingramcontent.com/pod-product-compliance
Lightning Source LLC
Chambersburg PA
CBHW021446070526
44577CB00002B/279